SMALL WOODEN BOATS

OF THE ATLANTIC

Small Wooden Boats

OF THE ATLANTIC

Photographs by Wayne Barrett • Text by David A. Walker

Introduction by Marven E. Moore

Nimbus Publishing Limited

Nimbus Publishing Limited
P.O. Box 9301, Station A
Halifax, Nova Scotia
B3K 5N5

Design: Steven Slipp, GDA, Halifax
Printing and binding: Everbest Printing Company, Limited, Hong Kong

Canadian Cataloguing in Publication Data

Barrett, Wayne.

Small wooden boats of the Atlantic

ISBN 0-921054-54-8

1. Wooden boats—Atlantic Provinces—Pictorial works.
2. Boat building—Atlantic
Provinces—History—Pictorial works. I. Walker, David
A. II. Title.

VM321.B37 1990   387.2'047   C90-097595-4

Frontispiece: **A small outboard-powered, round-bilge boat, Tidnish River, N.S.**

DEDICATION

In memory of RAY MACKEAN,
FRIEND, MENTOR, AND FELLOW
SMALL-WOODEN-BOAT LOVER

ACKNOWLEDGEMENTS

The photographer and the author would like to thank Marven E. Moore, for bringing them together; Niels Jannasch, for reading the manuscript; the late Johnny Williams, for his love of wooden boats; Noel O'Dea, Darlene Marshall, and Paul Lannon, for their hospitality; Regan Paquet of the P.E.I. Heritage Foundation, for his permission to photograph boats; Anne MacKay, for her encouragement and photographs; Tim Randall, for his photograph; and Shelley Campbell and Ron Gill, for their help in so many ways.

CONTENTS

INTRODUCTION

WAYNE BARRETT'S PHOTOGRAPHS of small wooden craft in Atlantic Canada represent a traditional approach to an uncommon subject. Even before the widespread use of the camera in the late nineteenth century, marine artists had for hundreds of years produced views of harbours, seascapes, and vessels. The artist's motivation ran the gamut from artistic challenge to financial reward. With the advent of the camera, views of these subjects not only became more accurate but also more commonplace. Wayne Barrett is therefore continuing a tradition established by marine artists and photographers from maritime nations around the world.

It is the subject of his photographs that is unique—small craft of Atlantic Canada. Compared with other aspects of maritime heritage, traditional small craft have been largely ignored by artists, photographers, and marine historians. Pictorial renderings, artifacts, and publications abound for larger vessels, particularly sailing ships. No doubt their romantic and spectacular images and the abundance of written records about them have made these vessels the favoured subject. In Atlantic Canada, libraries and archives have infinitely more material relating to large sailing ships of the last two centuries than they have relating to small craft—despite the fact that these boats played a constant and integral part in the evolution of our maritime economy and way of life.

Since the establishment of the earliest settlement, small craft have provided two crucial components in a marine environment: convenient transportation and a way to exploit the resources of the sea. They have fulfilled this role so effectively that they have become commonplace and, as a consequence, have been taken for granted.

Compared with other marine countries, particularly the United States and those in Europe, scant research, documentation, and writing has been directed towards small boats and their place in Atlantic Canada. In-depth studies and excellent publications have resulted from the dedicated work of Howard I. Chapelle and John Gardner in the United States, Eric MacKee in Great Britain, Christian Nielsen in Denmark, and Bernard Faeroyvik in Norway. Their efforts, together with those of many others, have generated a greater interest in small-craft preservation and traditional boat building in their respective countries.

To date, the same amount of attention has not been paid to Atlantic Canada's small craft. One of the few publications on the subject, and perhaps the best, is *The Little Boats: Inshore Fishing Craft of Atlantic Canada,* by Ray MacKean and Robert Percival (Brunswick Press, 1979). Their book, with its paintings, models, and research, is a valuable portrayal of traditional inshore fishing craft. Their hope of raising the consciousness of Atlantic Canadians to this forgotten part of our maritime heritage, however, is yet to be realized. Some valuable research has been initiated by one of their associates, David Walker. As a marine surveyor with an abiding interest in small craft, he has travelled throughout Atlantic Canada during the last 20 years, documenting the many types of

Facing page: **In Peggys Cove, N.S., the prominent colours of three St. Margarets Bay trap boats reflect in the water.**

This smart blue-and-white Cape Islander, the *Scotia Maid*, rests at a wharf in Brier Island, N.S.

Facing page: **The sculptured shape of the bow of the Strait boat distinguishes it from the Cape Islander. The twin rows of bumps, which look like rivets, are bolts securing the bilge stringers, the longitudinal stringers that give this boat much of her strength.**

boats. His narrative, therefore, provides a valuable insight into Wayne Barrett's collection of photographs.

The small craft featured in this book are representative of the recreational and commercial boats found in the four Atlantic provinces: New Brunswick, Nova Scotia, Prince Edward Island, and Newfoundland. Most are unpretentious vessels, scores of which can be seen tied to wharves or moorings, or pulled up on the shore of some harbour or river. Their design—simple in some

cases, more complex in others—have evolved over many years to meet the demands of local sailing conditions and particular functions. Their construction reflects the skills and traditions of generations of boat builders and seafarers whose craftsmanship and ingenuity enabled them to successfully confront the often-hazardous marine environment.

Boat builders and seafarers quickly learned which hull shape or form worked best in the environment in which the boat was to be used. The boats in these photographs reflect some of the ways craftsmen adapted their designs to meet these conditions. Forms of hulls range from flat bottom to long keel, square stem and stern to V-stem and transom stem, clinker to carvel planking. Each locality had its variations. A comparison of two similar hull shapes—the Cape Islander and the Strait boat—illustrates a subtle, but important, concession to local conditions. Unlike the Cape Islander, the Strait boat has a more pronounced flare at the bow to deflect the prevalent sea spray caused by the short, choppy waves of the Northumberland Strait and the Gulf of St. Lawrence.

The work a boat was expected to do had an equally important influence on its design. Fishing boats are one of the best examples of this. Flat-bottomed oyster boats and fishing punts, because of their shape, were ideally suited for use in inland rivers, streams, or estuaries. Their flat bottoms also made them stable work platforms for fishermen who had to stand in the boat either to rake the river bottom for oysters or to cast their fly rod. The flat bottom provided an accessible space

Wooden-boat-building yards can still be found throughout Atlantic Canada. This one is in Beach Point, P.E.I. This fine, small round-bottomed boat will soon be ready for turning over and finishing. The tools and equipment in the shop are as traditional as the boats they help create.

for their equipment and catch, making it easy to unload. Given the occasional or seasonal use of these vessels, the flat bottom also made it easier to haul them up on the shore after use.

Although the materials to build a boat do not affect its design as emphatically as local conditions and functions, they are extremely important in the construction and maintenance of the boat. Construction materials and methods have a direct impact on the cost of building and maintaining a boat. For the

owners of working boats, especially those of commercial fishermen, costs had to be kept to a minimum in order to maximize profits. To keep costs low, local wood was used whenever possible, as the availability made it cheaper to obtain. Even certain methods were adopted to hasten the construction process. The development of the dory clip used in the Shelburne dory, instead of the grown knee in the Lunenburg dory, facilitated speedier construction and obviated the need for grown knees, thereby keeping costs low. The philosophy that a working boat must be cheap to build and easy to maintain has, naturally, led commercial-boat builders and owners to adopt plywood and fibreglass as substitutes for traditionally built wooden boats.

As an industry, boat building evolved slowly. In the early part of the nineteenth century, boat building was carried on as an occasional or part-time occupation in coastal communities. Fishing or farming, or both, supplemented the boat builder's livelihood. As the population grew, urban centres developed and the fishing fleet expanded. By the beginning of this century, in Nova Scotia, for example, each county boasted at least a half dozen boat builders. Even today, boat building continues to be a mainstay of many coastal communities in the province. Names like Atkinson, Covey, D'Entremont, Embree, Etherington, Gray, Heisler, Kennedy, Langille, Levy, McAlpine, Stevens, and Theriault have been synonymous with Nova Scotian boat building during the past 100 years. A similar transition occurred in New

Brunswick, Prince Edward Island, and Newfoundland.

Traditionally, most boat-building operations were relatively modest in size and production, employing a small crew, building one or two vessels at a time. Some larger operations did emerge, especially those that built dories. Pressed to meet the incessant demand of the Grand Banks schooner fleet and inshore fishing, dory shops mass-produced vessels in great numbers. Using an early version of the assembly line, the John Williams Dory Shop, one of seven operating at the turn of this century on the waterfront in Shelburne, N.S., was able to produce approximately 250 dories per year with a crew of five to seven men.

Many of these businesses were family operations that had been passed from one generation to another. Not only were the firm and its reputation perpetuated in this way but also the skills, traditional methods, and local knowledge of boat design and construction. Boat building did not involve elaborate plans but instead relied on the use of a half-model, moulds, and rule-of-thumb. Details of the boat's construction were resolved between the builder and the buyer. Ironically, the verbal communication between these two principals is largely responsible for the lack of documentation about small boats. Consequently, much of the accumulated knowledge of these craft has faded from memory.

Although this book cannot retrieve this lost oral history, it does make an important contribution through its unique and authoritative view of some of this region's indigenous small craft. One hopes that it will encourage a greater interest in this vital component of Atlantic Canada's maritime heritage.

Marven E. Moore
Curator of Collections
Maritime Museum of the Atlantic
April 1990

Overleaf, right: **A dory fisherman checks his lobster traps in a Gros Morne fjord, Nfld., seemingly oblivious to his magnificent surroundings. His colour co-ordination is as smart as the best couturier's.**

SMALL WOODEN BOATS
OF THE ATLANTIC

THE ST. MARGARETS BAY TRAP BOAT

Facing page: **Sturdy St. Margarets Bay trap boats float in line formation at Fox Point, N.S. All except the closest boat are clinker built.**

This shade of green is the usual colour chosen by the fishermen of Fox Point. The bold sheer, emphasized by the shadows of the clinker planks, can be appreciated from this perspective.

AS YOU TRAVEL WEST along the Atlantic coast from Halifax, N.S., the first large bay you encounter is St. Margarets. Near the mouth of the bay lies picturesque Peggys Cove. In this tiny harbour, and in almost all the harbours in the bay, you can find trap boats.

The trap boats of Mill Cove, Fox Point, and Aspotogan are easily recognizable, as they are almost always green with black tarred interiors. They are large—up to 30 feet in length and 10 feet in breadth—heavy, and unpowered: often, several are towed in a

line by a fishing boat. They do not have sails, and they have only one or two short thwarts near the ends, where there is a single set of thole pins for rowing. Trap boats are carriers, used to haul heavy seines to fishing grounds and to return with loads of mackerel after the seines have been brailed out with dip nets.

Built from the 1890s to the 1950s, chiefly by the Covey family of St. Margarets Bay, trap boats are a microcosm of the two principal methods of wooden-boat building. Many are "clinker" built; that is, the planks overlap much like clapboards on a house. Others are smooth skinned, or "carvel" built; that is, the planks meet edge to edge. The clinker style of construction is known locally as lapwork, while the carvel style is known as seamwork. Both types of construction have adherents and detractors, but in St. Margarets Bay, examples of both work side by side.

There are also two designs. One type of trap boat is double ended, with a pointed stem at each end; the other has a graceful wineglass-shaped transom at the stern. All trap boats have a pronounced sheer, giving them an elegant profile. They have round hulls with gentle lines and have flat-plank or conventional keels. The wide beam, designed for carrying heavy loads, contributes to the pleasant overall appearance so often associated with Atlantic Canadian craft used for mundane chores.

The trap boat is, along with many other traditional craft, a vanishing type. Fortunately, it is a stout, sturdy vessel and should remain a feature of the St. Margarets Bay seascape for years to come.

FLAT-BOTTOMED BOATS

FLAT-BOTTOMED BOATS can be found anywhere in the Atlantic provinces, not to mention anywhere in the world. Because of their simple, straightforward construction, adaptability, and unassuming appearance, they are often overlooked as distinctive types. They are, however, worthy of more than a casual glance, as the inshore fishery and recreational fishing would be lost without them.

Flat-bottomed boats have been adapted for a variety of uses: providing transport from larger vessels anchored at moorings; oyster tonguing and mussel harvesting in Prince Edward Island; harvesting dulse; angling on rivers, streams, lakes, and estuaries; and teaching fundamental rowing, sailing, and boat building. In short, they can be used for almost anything in sheltered, calm waters.

This flat-bottomed boat is being rowed across the sheltered waters of Westport, Brier Island, N.S. Are the arrows there to give the oarsman a sense of direction?

Facing page: This clinker-built, flat-bottomed skiff in the sparkling waters off Chester, N.S., is well cared for. Note the thole pins attached to the gunwales ready for use; the transom has been strengthened to take a small outboard motor.

Simply built flat-bottomed boats sit on a skidway at Prospect, N.S. They are built of plywood, a material that lends itself to small, unsophisticated boats with plain, easy lines.

Facing page: Three flat-bottomed boats rest peacefully in the waters off Kouchibouguac National Park, N.B. Their obvious similarity means that they were probably built at the same boatshop. The far one is the "stretched" version of the others.

An old rubber boot has a second life as a practical bow fender on this rowboat, which has natural crook frames, band sawed from trees on which branches or roots carry the grain, and strengthened round corners.

Facing page: The boat in the foreground is used with an outboard motor. The lower blue stripe is a rail to clear spray when the boat is moving fast. A rowboat would not need one. The boat in the background, on the Walton, N.S., shingle flats has round bilges similar to a Cape Islander.

This huge skidway in York Harbour, Nfld., holds a group of round-bottomed boats pulled well away from the dangers of water and weather. The flat-bottomed craft in the foreground is reminiscent of a dory in the curve of the forward sheer and the type of construction.

Facing page: The owner of this bright little plywood craft in Ingomar, N.S., is not looking for passengers. If anyone wants to go along for a row, he will have to sit on the bottom. It may be a wet ride, however: the plastic bailer (an old bleach bottle) suggests that the boat may leak.

Chopper, a native of Lower Prospect, N.S., seems a somewhat ambitious name for a basic flat-bottomed boat. The owner has imagination and probably enjoys humorous comments about his outboard-powered craft. With no fittings for oars, it must be paddled when it runs out of fuel.

Facing page: A flat-bottomed boat with a transom at each end is usually called a "pram." The word comes from a Scandinavian one that describes similar craft in northern Europe. Prams are often used as yacht tenders. The major pieces of the smallest ones can be made from one sheet of four-foot-by-eight-foot plywood!

FLAT-BOTTOMED BOATS
THE OYSTER-TONGUING BOAT

The sparkling waters of West River, P.E.I., silhouette a lone oyster fisherman and his boat as he lowers his rake to the bottom in search of the succulent shellfish.

OYSTER-TONGUING BOATS are occasionally seen in Nova Scotia, along the Northumberland Shore, but their real home is Prince Edward Island, where they work the famous oyster beds of Malpeque Bay. There, fishermen row—the craft are usually unpowered—to their favourite areas, in sheltered waters close to shore.

Although the oyster-tonguing boat appears to be simply built with a pointed stem and a wide, flat bottom and transom, it has been adapted to suit its purpose in a variety of ways. Along the flat sides of the boat are strips of wood secured over the seams between the planks. These strips not only help keep the seams watertight but also protect the sides of the boat from wear and tear: the long oyster tongues, or poles, are repeatedly pushed to the bottom and withdrawn

The prongs of the oyster-tonguing rake remove shellfish from the sand, then one deft flick tips them into a small net that raises the oysters safely to the surface. (DAVID A. WALKER)

A flat-bottomed oyster-tonguing boat is moored fore and aft waiting for the next tide. The tilted tables on which the fisherman sorts his catch are on each side of the bow.

with their succulent catch. The rubbing strips themselves are easily and economically replaced.

On one or both sides of most of the boats, at the gunwales, are horizontal planks with low sides. Fishermen place their dredgings on these "tables," then quickly sort the oysters, discarding the refuse and putting the select mature bivalves into waiting buckets. The sorting tables are at the bow or stern of the boat, depending on the fisherman's preference and even whether he is right or left

handed. (Whether a fisherman is right or left handed determines the detail design or fittings of a number of different types of Atlantic Canadian boats: for instance, some boats on the north shore of Nova Scotia have lobster-trap haulers on the starboard; most others have them on the port side near the aft end. In all regions, some craft have steering wheels on the port side of the shelter or wheelhouse.)

The tongue used to dredge the oyster beds is one of the most unusual pieces of fishing equipment used anywhere. It is built from two long, slender spruce poles that are bolted together so that they function much like a pair of scissors. The business end of each pole resembles the end of an ordinary garden rake, though the tonguing rake is longer and has more teeth. Operating a tonguing rake requires a certain amount of skill. The fisherman stands in his boat, grips the end of each pole, and scoops a portion of the bed between the teeth. Then he closes the poles and lifts the contents onto the sorting tables. Working blind, he uses his knowledge and experience to judge the effectiveness of his raking.

Oyster-tonguing boats—usually 12 to 16 feet long and built of spruce or, more recently, plywood—are pleasing to the eye. One may be examined at the Basin Head Fisheries Museum in eastern Prince Edward Island. It is typical in shape and detail and size, but the original owner was enterprising and fitted it with a small inboard engine.

FLAT-BOTTOMED BOATS
THE MUSSEL-HARVESTING BOAT

Facing page: **Mussel farming is a growth industry in many parts of Atlantic Canada. The neat rows of buoys on this farm in Murray Harbour, P.E.I., are reminiscent of a dirt farm with its neat rows of produce. The buoys support the mussel strings. The harvesting boats lie at their nearby moorings.**

THE FARMING OF cultivated mussels is a relatively new industry in Atlantic Canada. It is a reliable alternative to harvesting wild mussels and is now an established means of producing a continuous crop of fat, sand-free shellfish for dinner tables across the country. The mussels are grown on strings or in stocking-like nets slung from lines running along the surface of sheltered bays and inlets. This is a simple way of describing what is a complex process that begins with collecting spat, or baby mussels, and encouraging them to grow, first on trays, then on the lines. After two or three years, they are harvested, sorted, washed, and cleaned with specially designed equipment.

The industry could not function without specially designed boats to carry the heavy produce. Mussel-harvesting boats are not traditional or handsome: they are burdensome, ungainly, and clumsy-looking workhorses. Highly functional, they are perhaps best described as pickup trucks of the sea.

The mussel-harvesting boat looks like a barge. About 8 feet wide, 20 feet long, and 2-1/2 feet deep, it is heavily built and strongly framed and braced so that it can carry stacks of boxes of mussels—a lesser craft would swamp under the weight. The stern is not much different from the bow, but a sharp eye can detect a slightly greater rake, or slope, to the bow. At the stern, there is an outboard motor; at the bow, there is a small hydraulic hauler that pulls the lines out of the water and to within the grasp of the harvesters. There is sometimes a small davit near the hauler that lifts the lines higher and makes it a little easier to clear the tenaciously clinging mussels from the strings.

The mussel-harvesting boat is an unassuming craft. It is never in a hurry and always works in calm waters close to shore.

The boat used to harvest mussels is not attractive or complex. But it is practical, and well designed for its purpose. The crew collects mussels from the lines and stows them in boxes for delivery to the cleaning and washing plant onshore.

FLAT-BOTTOMED BOATS
THE EEL-FISHING BOAT

This odd-shaped device is used to catch eels in appropriately named Eel Brook, N.S. It is weighted down with stones and put on the stream bed. Then the trap lures the eels into a path from which there is no escape. This type of trap is similar to the ones made by native peoples. (DAVID A. WALKER)

Right: Colourful puntlike craft are used in the eel fishery on the Miramichi River at Chatham, N.B.

Facing page: Eel fishermen working on the Saint John River near Woodstock, N.B., pull an eel trap net into their small puntlike boat. The seat is actually a fishwell that keeps the catch alive: eels are often marketed live. (ANNE MACKAY)

THE LIFE CYCLE OF American eels is opposite to that of salmon. Eels hatch and live the first part of their lives in the Sargasso Sea, then return to their parental freshwater home for some years before returning to the Sargasso Sea to restart the cycle.

Eels are fished in numerous rivers and streams of eastern Canada and, as in the past, are caught in traps. Some traps are set in stream banks or small rivers, and fishermen work them wearing waders. Other traps, however, are set in larger, deeper waters, and fishermen need boats to retrieve their catch. The craft are all similar in appearance: they are usually flat-bottomed, puntlike boats with a ramp bow and flat sides.

Eel-fishing boats are not sophisticated in design, as they do not have to carry large loads, navigate rough waters, or travel fast. All they have to do is transport their owners to their traps, then take them periodically to empty the traps and carry the catch ashore, where it is kept in holding boxes until it is marketed.

The traps, in fact, are more complicated in construction than the boats. Native peoples made woven withy traps to catch the lean, elusive delicacies and, until recently in Nova Scotia, were still weaving traps for their own use and for sale. Today's trap has changed little in design but is now made from metal wire and netting.

FLAT-BOTTOMED BOATS
THE CATTLE FERRY

IN ATLANTIC CANADA, specialized craft have been developed to meet all kinds of needs. Among the most specialized is the cattle ferry, used on the Saint John River, N.B.

Along the river, there are many islands that flood every spring. The farmers who live on the banks have long used these islands for grazing their cattle in summer and fall. To transport their animals to and from these lush "water meadows," the farmers use ferries. No one knows how long boats have been used for this purpose: in earlier days, perhaps, cat-

tle had to swim back and forth, but obviously, that practice was hazardous.

Each cattle ferry is built to suit the requirements and the purse of the farmer. Simple decked-over scows with a railing along the sides and a rope or gate at each end, they usually carry 6 to 10 heads of cattle. Propulsion is elementary. An underwater cable or rope runs from the mainland to the island. The farmer lifts the cable from the bottom and pulls on the cable hand over hand, dragging the boat from side to side.

Farmers living along the Saint John River, N.B., use island "meadows" to graze their cattle in summer and fall.

Facing page: This is a tranquil scene on the Saint John River at McGowans Corner, N.B. This ferry is used for the sole purpose of transporting livestock to "water meadows" along the river. The small boat on the far side is possibly towing it.

FLAT-BOTTOMED BOATS
THE TUB PUNT

Facing page: This rugged little double-ended boat, at Tiverton, N.S., is typical of those found on the islands at the end of Digby Neck. Tub punts are rarely seen today, as they are no longer being built. This boat carries a plastic tub used to hold a long-line trawl. (DAVID A. WALKER)

The stout construction of this tub punt can be seen in the size of her frames and heavy knees. The rub rails at the top and bottom protect against damage when transferring cargo in choppy waters.

THE TUB PUNT was common up to 15 years ago in Nova Scotia, along Digby Neck, especially in the villages near the western end. This small craft, however, is no longer being built and has almost disappeared from the area. The origin of its name is obscure—often the case with locally built and used craft—but one thing is certain, it does not resemble a punt in any way and is never used like a punt.

The word "tub," on the other hand, does relate to its function. Tub punts, towed by fishing vessels, were originally built to carry tubs of longline trawls back and forth to fishing grounds. In this way, fishing boats could take more baited trawl lines and, it was hoped, return with more catch. The tub punt was stoutly constructed to withstand the rough weather and the abuse of loading and unloading that its job entailed.

Flat bottomed, tub punts may be loosely compared to double-ended dories. But they do not have the elegant sheer and are much heavier in construction, with bigger frames and thicker planking. Tub punts have thwarts and thole pins near the ends, but neither outboard nor inboard motors can be fitted to these double-ended boats. They are conspicuously equipped with a low, heavy towing ring at the stem—the easiest way to distinguish bow from stern in these almost-symmetrical vessels. The bottoms are reinforced with an extra sheathing of hardwood, as the boats are often beached or hauled up launching ramps, prevalent in this region of high tides.

These unglamorous workhorses of the fishing industry were usually about 14 to 16 feet in length, with a tubby breadth of 4 feet or more. They were locally built from North Mountain spruce, and their builders remain as inconspicuous as the boats are now becoming. The tub punt will soon vanish, another traditional wooden craft that was as common 30 or 40 years ago as its fibreglass and aluminum replacements are today.

An upside-down tub punt shows the extra hardwood planking on the bottom, which is ready for replacement. The towing shackle is fitted low on the stem for easier tracking.

THE DORY

IF ANY SMALL BOAT is the symbol of the Atlantic region, it is the dory. It graces every cove, inlet, harbour, and fishing village throughout Atlantic Canada—in fact, all along the New England coast as well. The dory is truly ubiquitous.

It cannot be claimed as an invention of the region, however, for small craft that are virtually indistinguishable from the dory exist in various European countries. Nonetheless, Atlantic Canadians have made it their own.

In eastern Canada, the dory is almost always painted a distinctive yellow-brown known as dory buff. The boat comes in several sizes and is usually measured along the length of its bottom. The actual overall length, however, is about four feet more, as the fore and the aft each slope out at approximately the same angle for about two feet.

The dory appears to be simple in construction, yet, like many man-made things, it is a carefully developed combination of design, materials, and use. It is built from native wood, and other local materials are used

A traditionally painted, powered dory off McCallum, Nfld., has a retracting propeller and shaft so that it can be hauled up a slipway or beach without being damaged. The fisherman is steering with tiller ropes so that he can adjust the engine and steer without moving around.

Facing page: **A dory rests at the edge of the tide line at Dark Harbour, Grand Manan Island, N.B. Dark Harbour is known for its dulse, and the parting boards beneath the thwarts of this boat indicate that it is used to collect this lucrative seaweed.**

Facing page: This dory is a workboat on a fishing vessel at Digby, N.S. One hopes that it is not needed quickly, as its real use is as a stowage locker. Lifesaving is the job of the inflatable boat in the white canister on the other side of the deckhouse.

The paraphernalia of the fishing business is not always dull, proved by these colourful buoys sitting on a wharf at Lower West Pubnico, N.S. The stacked lobster traps indicate that the season is about to start or has just finished.

wherever possible. The hull is flat bottomed with generously flared sides that ensure that the heavier the load the more stable the boat becomes. The bottom is rockered, and pointed at each end, though the hull has a transom that is called a "tombstone" after its unique shape. The flared sides are planked with partially overlapping seams, forming a strong lengthwise joint that tapers out at the ends. This seam is known in the boat-building world as the dory lap.

The dory probably first came to the north-east coast in the late sixteenth century, with the Basques and the French who fished here during summer. There is evidence to show that they brought boats as cargo atop the salt in the holds of their ships.

The dory has never left. It became most popular during the nineteenth century, when the Grand Banks schooner fishery was at its peak. Each schooner carried many dories aboard and became mother ship to a fleet of small boats whose two-man crews handlined for cod and halibut.

At that time, the dory was "manufactured." In Nova Scotia and New England, workshops literally mass-produced dories on an early form of assembly line. Skilled employees cut the various components from precise patterns, while others assembled the craft to meet the continuous demand from the Grand Banks and the inshore fishermen. In addition, innumerable small boatshops custom-made dories to individual orders.

One unique feature of the dory made it suitable for the schooner fishery and for manufacturing. Dories can be nested on top of each other by simply removing the thwarts. Schooners, therefore, could carry large numbers of dories when heading out to sea, and factories could ship several at a time within the floor area of one.

Today, dories have fallen out of general use: the Banks dory fleet has vanished, fishing boats that used the dory as a lifeboat have switched to the more compact inflatable life raft, and inshore fishermen have chosen a bigger craft because the dory cannot be easily converted to power. There are no more dory

Fishermen are practical, as this simple ladder illustrates. At Sandy Cove, N.S., the high Fundy tides sometimes make rocks slippery. This ladder makes the climb easier and safer.

factories, and only a few isolated builders produce occasional boats for enthusiastic owners.

Still, some can be found. The queen of the dory fleet is in St. Pierre and Miquelon. A large boat with an exaggerated upper sheer and a long tombstone, it is truly magnificent and has a reputation among the French for safety, reliability, and great capacity.

The two principal types in Nova Scotia are the Lunenburg dory and the Shelburne dory. To the casual observer, they look almost identical. A closer look, however, reveals that the Shelburne vessel has slightly more sheer and flare than her Lunenburg sister. The most significant difference is, the Lunenburg dory is built with natural crook frames; that is, the frame is one piece of wood sawed from a natural growth where the root or branch of a tree takes the grain in a natural sweep or curve. Shelburne builders, however, did not go to the trouble to select such timbers. They formed frames from two pieces of wood connected at the chine by two galvanized metal clips riveted through each structural member. The clip was invented and patented by a Shelburne native, Coffin Crowel.

Another variety is the Shelburne clipper dory. It has curved sides and has almost always been fitted with sails and centreboards and used for recreational sailing. It is similar in appearance to a craft common in New England, the Swampscott dory, named after the town where it was developed.

It is no wonder that Atlantic Canadians have romanticized the dory. Books have been written about these boats—about their many uses and guises and about the brave men who have sailed in them. They have been sailed across the Atlantic, and they have found their way to the West Coast, where they have been used in the halibut fishery. Dories have been fitted with outboard motors, inboard engines, and sails and centreboards, and they have been developed into variations that have gained adherents of their own.

The grandeur of the cliffs at François, Nfld., over-shadow a working dory.

Overleaf, left: The thwarts on this Shelburne dory have been removed, making it easy to see the clips that join the frames to the floor. The boat may have been used for lifesaving, as there is reflective safety tape at the gunwales.

Overleaf, right: A dory basks in the sheltered back-water near Weymouth, N.S.

WATERFOWL-HUNTING CRAFT

This basic, unpretentious boat may be used for waterfowl hunting. The owner wanted a slow-moving, low-cost craft that carried large returns. He got it.

EVERY FALL, hunters throughout Atlantic Canada follow their favourite waterfowl, using decoys to lure birds into their sight. They usually hunt out of camouflaged blinds built in the marshes or from boats that are unusual and varied.

Hunting waterfowl was not always a sport: early immigrants and native peoples hunted land and water birds out of necessity. Others hunted for cash, beginning in the spring, when the first birds arrived in the north, and finishing in the fall, when the last birds headed south.

Generally, there are three types of hunting craft: aluminum boats, bought at supply houses or through catalogues, which owners paint in dull camouflage colours to hide the glare; general-purpose wooden or fibreglass boats that are similar to the metal ones; and specialized boats that are developed truly for waterfowl hunting.

The third type consists of one-man hand-cranked, paddle-wheel, or propeller-powered goose or sneak boats, and duck boats with side coamings like small blinds that can be raised as required after paddling to location.

These boats cannot possibly be used for anything but waterfowl hunting. They were common in the market-hunting days. The goose boats, with raised sides covered with ice in the spring to make floating mini-icebergs, were ultimately declared illegal, and many were burned by the RCMP.

Facing page: **A little coffin-like boat was used to hunt ducks in the waters of P.E.I. The craft is a sink boat and can be seen at the Basin Head Fisheries Museum. A hunter sunk a series of them near the tide line and moved from one to the next as the tide rose or fell.**

THE ST. MARYS RIVERBOAT

Facing page: **These colourful punts on the St. Marys River, N.S., are used in the upriver reaches and pools. Fitted with outboard brackets, they are shorter than the riverboats found near Sherbrooke. (TIM RANDALL)**

Punting is an ancient art. Briefly, the pole is pushed to the riverbed and used as a lever to force the craft forward. It is a subtle combination of leg, arm, and trunk co-ordination. This angler makes it look easy as he poles to a better location.

SALMON ANGLERS on eastern Nova Scotia's St. Marys River cast their flies with artistic flourishes, testing their skills as they sit or stand in long, slender, shallow punts called "riverboats." These deceptively simple craft have been used for as long as anyone can remember. St. Marys River settlers probably began building punts when they found enough time for recreational fishing and boat building. For example, there was a puntlike ferry at Sherbrooke in 1819, when Lord Dalhousie visited the area: military artist Major J.E. Woolford, Lord Dalhousie's companion, sketched the craft at that time.

Before sawmills supplied planks, settlers made dugouts from logs. The long, narrow shape of the dugouts was well suited to the shallow, swift waters of the St. Marys River. Therefore, when settlers began building riverboats, they imitated the shape. Subtle changes are continually made to traditional craft, though boats appear to remain static in form. As boats grow old and are replaced, owners tend to incorporate small, imperceptible alterations based on experience or observation. These changes no doubt make boats safer. In the case of riverboats, anglers have less chance of tipping overboard than their predecessors.

The type of riverboat seen today is much wider and has less-vertical sides. It was first built from two long spruce side planks with ramps cut at each end, the fore ramp being about two times longer than the aft ramp. The bottom was then cross-planked with pine boards, sometimes tongue-and-groove flooring planks. Local spruce, used for the sides, provided strength, while the pine, used for the bottom, withstood the wet and dry conditions encountered seasonally.

The bow of the riverboat is wider than the stern, as anglers believe that a narrow bow will yaw in swift currents. The relatively wide bow and the long ramp also allow for easier entry. Stern widths, on the other hand, are usually determined by the weight of the owner: he needs the correct amount of buoyancy to support him while keeping the punt balanced on an even trim. He always stands near the stern when poling upriver, and when fly casting, he usually stands or sits near the centre.

Used in various parts of the world, punts are propelled with a long pole thrust into the river bottom and used as a lever for the angler to push against. This skill is learned and practised to perfection, as the pole may stick to the bottom and pull the operator overboard or may get lost. Expert anglers, in fact, can actually hold a riverboat still with the pole under their arm while casting. Some anglers now paddle their punts, while some others have fitted theirs with small transoms for outboard motors.

Riverboats, about 20 to 22 feet long on the lower stretches of the St. Marys, are also held stationary by an unusual anchor made from a small bundle of iron chain. Flexible, the bunch conforms to the rocky river bottom without snagging like a traditional fluked anchor. The anchor is held over the bow of the punt on a tiny davit and pulley. The anchor rope is attached to the stern, where the angler poles, so that he can loosen the rope from its cleat and drop anchor with the least amount of movement.

A 20-foot-long plywood riverboat waits along the bank of the St. Marys near Sherbrooke Village. The punting pole and the bailer are inside. All the angler needs to do is bring his rod and cast off. (DAVID A. WALKER)

Facing page: This new riverboat at Silver's Pool, on the St. Marys River, is unique, as it has been built with traditional wooden planking, not plywood. The narrow stern is easy to detect. (DAVID A. WALKER)

THE TUSKET RIVER SQUARE-ENDER

Facing page: Unlike the St. Marys River punts, the Tusket River square-enders are not used entirely for pleasure. In the appropriate seasons, they are used to fish for gaspereaux or eels. These punts are shorter and wider than the other craft and have side and bottom frames.

THE TUSKET RIVER is another Nova Scotia angling gem. Sport fishermen flock to this well-known stream, near the western end of the province, to challenge the wily Atlantic salmon. They often fish in a type of punt that has evolved along this river. It has the unglamorous name "square-ender."

The square-enders do not resemble the angling punts on any other river in Nova Scotia. They are shorter, wider, and deeper and often do not have seats. Consequently, they are built and also shaped differently than their cousins. They perhaps resemble scows more than punts, as they have a definite stem transom that slopes at a greater angle than the usual stern transom. The sides of the boats are flared outwards more than the others and have two planks, either clinker or carvel built. Bottoms of the older square-enders were fore and aft planked like dories, and this means that the boats had to have frames to hold them together. The other punts, with transverse planing and a one-sided plank, do not need frames.

Tradition has retained frames in the Tusket square-enders today, even though many are now built of plywood. They are usually made from three pieces of wood joined at the chine by plywood brackets. The occasional boat, however, does have double frames with naturally grown timber knees.

Square-enders vary in length from 12 to 18 feet and in width from 30 inches to 4 feet. In addition to being used for sport fishing, they are used in the eel fishery, a seasonal pursuit on the Tusket River. They can be poled, and some transoms have been reinforced to take an outboard motor. Those square-enders with seats often have thole pins so that they can be rowed.

The frames are evident in this empty square-ender, and it is also clear why they are fitted: the boat has a vertically planked bottom, not cross-planked as in other punts. The difference between the bow and stern slopes is also clear.

THE GANDER RIVERBOAT

An upturned riverboat shows that the craft is not simply a canoe with a chopped-off stern. Its stern has a small skeg and transom specifically designed for an engine; it also has a more distinct keel than a canoe.

THE NATIVE PEOPLES of Newfoundland were the first to build the antecedent to this boat: the river canoe. Early European settlers no doubt used the native craft and must have noted all the advantages.

Centuries later, with a little imagination, one can see the river canoe in the lines and curves of today's boats. The native influence can also be detected in the method of propulsion—when the outboard motor cannot be used, the boats are paddled—and in the size. The boats are long for a river canoe,

between 16 and 24 feet, suggesting that the original craft may have been used as seagoing vessels. They rarely exceed more than 30 to 36 inches in breadth.

But a lot has changed. The present-day boat is almost totally European in construction, from the stem frame to the tiny vertical transom, which appears to be a recent concession to the ubiquitous outboard motor. The overall framing of some riverboats resembles the wide, flat hackmatack framing of native craft, but the planking is thicker and does not require a top layer of bark or hide to keep out the water. Other differences include the more prominent keel and the small forward deck. The deck will afford a modest dry space within the hull, and it will probably be needed, as the bow is lower than that of the native craft, creating a tendency to ship water over the stem when negotiating rapids.

Gander riverboats play many roles: guide boats for hunters, trappers, and fishermen; supply boats for camps and cottages; transport boats along the winding Gander River; and tourboats for an increasing number of people visiting the wilderness areas of the interior of Newfoundland.

Facing page: An elegant riverboat from Gander, Nfld., has fine lines and moves through the water with little effort. It is easy to see the descent from a native canoe in the shape and construction, though the riverboat was built in a more rugged fashion. It has a paddle and an outboard motor. It can also be poled like a punt.

THE MIRAMICHI RIVERBOAT

Facing page: **Four riverboats on the Miramichi River, N.B., wait for a day of fishing.**

Anglers get an early morning start from the Miramichi Salmon Club, in Doaktown, N.B. The guide poles the boat quietly in the shallow waters, ignoring the outboard. The bundle of chain used as an anchor hangs ready at the bow.

THE FISHING BOATS of the Miramichi Salmon Club, at Doaktown, N.B., are distant cousins of the Gander riverboats. There are differences, but a glance at the shape of these two boats show that they share the same ancestors. In many ways, the New Brunswick boat is a closer relative of the canoe, for it not only has the general shape but also a similar type of construction. This boat is, in reality, still a canoe.

The Miramichi riverboat has copied the form of the large freight canoe used by European explorers when they penetrated the

Canadian wilderness with Indians as guides. The bigger European craft could carry huge cargoes into the back country, where they traded goods for furs. Today, the Miramichi descendant performs less-exciting duties—unless you are an enthusiastic angler and manage to land one of the region's famous salmon.

Miramichi riverboats are well suited to angling. The comfortable seats, for two anglers, are set quite high, a testimony to the canoe's stability—sitting so high in many canoes would mean an instant dip. The boats are 20 feet long or longer yet have been shortened a bit in recent years so that a transom could be built at the stern to fit an outboard motor. As an alternative to the outboard motor, when tranquillity is desired, these craft can be paddled, or poled in shallow waters.

The guide who steers the craft to little-known corners of the river sits near the stern on a traditional woven wicker thwart. He also controls the anchor, which holds the boat in position in the swifter waters. This anchor is similar to that used by the St. Marys River punts—a small bundle of chain.

The boats are built mostly of cedar, with a canvas covering similar to that used by Europeans when they built their version of the native canoe. After the thin planks are laid over the almost equally thin ribs, the canvas is stretched and doped to make a strong, light, watertight, and pliable craft that will give a little in turbulent waters. This allows the craft to follow broken rapids, rather than remain rigid and fight choppy waves.

The long, lean lines of the Miramichi riverboat can be appreciated from this angle.

Facing page: A Miramichi riverboat looks like a canoe with the stern cut off. The anchor is on the riverbed, the rope safely cleated near the guide's right hand. The punting pole is handy; only anglers are needed to complete the picture.

THE CAPE ISLAND BOAT

Facing page: The crew of a Cape Islander stand nonchalantly on the deck as the hull tosses aside the choppy offshore waters. The forerunners of this hardy boat have been warding off waters like these for some 80 years.

Two fishermen in their small Cape Islander return to Herring Cove, N.S. The boat is equipped for lobstering, with the snatch block on the shelter top and the hydraulic trap hauler at the skipper's right hand.

Overleaf, left: The deeply laden *Cape Smokey* has brought a catch of mackerel into Ingonish, Cape Breton Island. This is a typical Cape Islander found east of Halifax: it has an open cockpit forward of the small shelter.

Overleaf, right: The *Lucky Strike IV*, of Little River Harbour, N.S., has a typically high bow. It also has a full deckhouse shelter and cuddy, two radars, and an inflatable life raft.

THE CAPE ISLAND BOAT—or the Cape Islander, as it is more commonly known—is a true example of Nova Scotia boat-building expertise. The boat was developed on Cape Sable Island about the turn of the century, when engines were first being used by small fishing vessels. Its designer was Ephram Atkinson, a resident of Clark's Harbour who had been building sailing vessels for several years.

At the time, Atkinson realized that the small gasoline engine was going to revolutionize inshore fishing craft, and he set out to produce an efficient boat. It soon became apparent, however, that his sailing hull design was not suitable for gasoline engines. Any new design would have to take into account the size and weight of the engine and its fuel. Simply fitting an engine onto a sailing craft was not the answer.

The original craft was somewhat different from those called Cape Islanders today. Yet Atkinson's pedigree can still be detected. His boat was long and slender, with a saucy sheer

towards the forward end and a gently round-ed stem; the transom was flat and almost ver-tical, except for a slight forward lean. An open boat at first, it was soon fitted with a small forward cuddy and later a windshield. The boat's hull, however, was the most unique aspect of Atkinson's design. It had a sharp forward entry with a cutaway forefoot and a long, smooth run to the stern, where the lines of the bottom ran almost flat to the gentle curve of the side bilges.

This nearly revolutionary form gave the Cape Islander a tremendous ability to move easily through the water with only moderate power while carrying a load of fish. Although the boat did have to be handled with more care when it was loaded—there was reduced freeboard—experienced fishermen did not think this was a problem.

Since the time the boat was designed, it has found its way into every port in Atlantic Canada. Many have been exported to New England, where a similar boat, the Jonesport,

Fashion and fads are as apparent in boats as they are in clothes and cars. The mast antennae on all these Meteghan, N.S., boats are becoming popular, as are the forward sloping windows in the wheel-houses of the second and the fourth from the left.

Facing page: **This Cape Islander on the beach at Parrsboro, N.S., is having her hull painted. The unique lines of this craft can be appreciated from this angle. The deep "V" slowly eases out and aft until the underwater section at the stern is almost flat out to the bilges.**

has been developed. The originator of the Jonesport boat, it is believed, was an expatriate Nova Scotian boat builder who went to the Boston States during the First World War.

The present-day Cape Islander has the same deep V-shaped hull at the forward end and the same long, easy run aft to a flat underwater hull at the stern. It also has the same cutaway forefoot, for easy turning, and a well-protected propeller under the wide, flat transom. In many ways, however, the newer boats depart from the original design.

The Cape Islander is now much wider and has an extreme forward sheer to the stem, which is almost always vertical. It has a full shelter, a deckhouse with complete weather protection, a larger forward cuddy with sleeping capacity and cooking facilities—all in a craft much bigger than that first envisioned by Ephram Atkinson (it has grown from 26 feet to more than 50).

Wooden Cape Islanders are becoming an endangered species, as they are now almost always built of fibreglass-reinforced plastic. It is nevertheless remarkable that fishermen still cling to the original shape, even though the boats are bigger, more powerful, and stay out at sea for much longer periods. The conservative fisherman demands a vessel he knows and trusts.

Although in Ketch Harbour, N.S., this small Cape Islander, with its open forward cockpit and tiny shelter, is typical of eastern-shore craft.

Facing page: These fishing boats at Meteghan, N.S., are not true Cape Islanders, but their heritage is obvious. They are bigger and operate farther offshore and for longer periods. They have been fitted with much more elaborate fishing gear than their smaller cousins.

Little Shell awaits spring on the snowy shores of
Rocky Harbour, Nfld., far away from her birthplace
in Clark's Harbour, N.S., the legendary ancestral
home of all Cape Islanders. Her lines and bright
yellow paint belie her 21 years of fishing.

Facing page: Two lobster boats whose ancestry is
plain wait for new spring coats of paint and for the
ice to leave the Gulf of St. Lawrence.

THE STRAIT BOAT

Facing page: **To appreciate a Strait boat, look at one when it is upside-down. The complex curves contrasting the straight horizon line are almost surrealistic.**

A Northumberland Strait lobster boat sits on her cradle in a field near Pugwash, N.S. She needs a little attention from her owner: rusting nails outline her ribs.

THE MOST COMMON TYPE of inshore fishing vessel on Prince Edward Island can also be found along the Northumberland shores of New Brunswick and Nova Scotia. It has various names, such as "Strait boat" or "wedge boat." The first, of course, comes from its locale; the second comes from the prominent "V," or wedge, shape of the bow.

At first glance, these boats, usually white and about 35 to 40 feet long, seem to resemble Cape Islanders, but a closer inspection reveals that there are many differences. The Strait boat has a much gentler upper sheer, without any raised forecastle or exaggerated upward thrust at the stem. The curve continues along the entire sheer, and many believe it is more attractive. The stem is vertical, but the hull sides near the bow have a wide flare. This feature gives the boat a spacious forecastle deck. Although the deck is used only to moor or tie up the boat, the wide flare does serve an important purpose in the short, choppy waters of the Northumberland Strait and the Gulf of St. Lawrence: it throws the sea spray well away from the bow and allows fishermen to work in dry conditions on the aft part of the vessel.

The unusual construction of the hull allowed for the design of the flare. Wooden Strait boats were always built of edge-nailed planks that are narrow—only a little wider than they are thick—and almost square. The origin of this method is unknown, but it enabled the builder to form sharper curves. (At the bow near the tip of the wide flare, the planks are actually narrower than they are thick.) The design has received such acceptance, in fact, that builders now making these boats in fibreglass faithfully duplicate the shape.

Strait boats have other distinguishing features. Sometimes used by lobster fishermen, they have haulers at the aft end, formerly mechanically driven by the engine but usually hydraulic today. Two fishermen work in each boat and haul up their lines of lobster traps and arrange them along the rail of the boat. In addition, many boats are fitted with elaborate shelters and small cuddies, though not

too long ago, the boats were open. The shelters have uneven sloping windows that slope forward at the top and aft at the bottom, helping reduce the sun's glare. The cuddies do not have elaborate sleeping and cooking facilities, as Strait boats rarely stay out fishing for more than a day at a time.

Nor do they fish in winter, for the Northumberland Strait and Gulf of St. Lawrence waters freeze over. The boats are hauled ashore on special trailers and routinely spend the winter in the backyards of their owners being serviced and repaired. During this time, the remarkable "V" shape at the bow is visible. So is the flat aft end, with its long, easy run to the transom—one similarity to the Cape Islander—and the keel, which is long and straight from the rudder to the vertical stem.

It is not easy to trace the forebears of these boats, as they bear no resemblance to their sailing ancestors, called "pinkies." The pinky, predominant in the nineteenth and early twentieth centuries, had an unusual transom and two masts and was schooner rigged. A few years ago, the fishermen of Northport, N.S., still called their round-sterned Strait boats pinkies, but no round-sterned boats can be seen today.

Her fishing days over, her graceful sheer twisted out of existence, this derelict Strait boat lies forlornly on the beach at Parrsboro, N.S. The pointed stern was often found on these boats but is now seldom seen. The frames and the last vestiges of the bow flare can be noted.

Facing page: The still waters of Murray Harbour, P.E.I., reflect the curves of these typical Strait boats. The craft can be seen in every port in summer and in many backyards in winter, when they are hauled out of the water away from crippling ice.

During a blessing of the fleet, fishermen, their families, and their friends clean and decorate their boats and sail past clergy, who give their blessing for a safe, bountiful harvest. The crowd aboard 5211 seem to be caught up in the spirit of the event.

Facing page: The *David Wayne II* and companion are loading lobster traps at the start of another season of fishing the bountiful waters around P.E.I. These craft can carry more than 200 traps.

NEWFOUNDLAND FISHING BOATS

A Newfoundland fishing boat puts into Holyrood. The fine lines of this graceful vessel, seen in the bold curve of the transom and wide-flaring bow, show a seaworthy craft well suited to her purpose. Her tender in matching red paint follows dutifully astern.

THE BOATS OF Newfoundland have many features that set them apart from small inshore craft found elsewhere along the eastern seaboard. They are well suited to the unique climatic and sea conditions of the island and have made the transition from sail to power with fewer changes than many other small boats.

According to the American historian Howard I. Chapelle, Newfoundland fishing boats are descendants of yawl boats, carried over the transom of early fishing schooners and trading vessels, or of a Nova Scotia boat introduced about 1870. Chapelle, however, ignores the fact that Newfoundlanders come from a long line of English, Scottish, Irish, and French sailors and fishermen who brought their own boat-building traditions to the New World. These traditions can easily be detected in various features of present-day Newfoundland fishing vessels.

The boats have numerous names—trap boats, skiffs, whalers, Toulinget (the original name for Twillingate) boats, and others—many of which are regional in origin. But the boats are essentially similar, even though they probably have a greater range of sizes than Cape Islanders.

Two early influences, perhaps, were the New England boats that fished the Grand Banks and that were used in sealing and whaling fleets. Both of these early types were double-ended boats, but there are few vestiges of double-ended craft left on Newfoundland, except in the fine underwater lines and the still-popular external rudder. New England boats were almost always clinker built, but besides small craft, this type of construction is now uncommon on the island.

The larger Newfoundland fishing boats have complete decks, engine "rooms," fish

Facing page: Resting quietly in Ferryland, Nfld., is a typical small fishing boat found almost everywhere on the island. The classic curve of the upsweeping stem is reminiscent of the early Nova Scotian schooners, but it is actually European in origin.

holds, forecastles, and deckhouses almost worthy of much bigger offshore fishing vessels. The smaller inshore vessels, with their "powder-horn" sheer, have less-complete decks with limited space for amenities; they are also open and are propelled by outboard motors or oars. Some are equipped for sculling, through a hole in the transom.

The large and small boats usually have broad cross-sections with fine ends, making them at once burdensome and easy to manoeuvre. They always have a full, elegant transom that often turns in gracefully at the top. The transom can slope at various angles, depending on the boat. The angle is not determined by any apparent pattern: large and small have everything from vertical transoms to sloping sterns. All are fine at the waterline.

The typical medium-sized inshore fishing vessel has a partially decked hull forming fish compartments, a low coaming or rail, and a small deckhouse or wheelhouse near the aft end. These are the essential elements, but within this broad description is a group of boats that vary as much as the imaginations, the skills, and the talents of their owners and builders.

The medium-sized boats have flair: no-nonsense Nova Scotian vertical stems and

As time goes by, fewer and fewer large boats are being built in Newfoundland. One of these fine examples of fishing craft was built in Newfoundland, though the trade has all but disappeared on the island.

Boats in Bonavista Bay show the similarities between boats of different sizes in Newfoundland, even in the choice of colours. The reels on the boats are used to jig for squid—no more hand-jigging.

transoms have no place on these craft, which sport sharply curved stems that rise from the water with an eager forward curve. The transoms are sloped, and when viewed from behind, they look graceful, almost heartlike in shape. The bold sheers of the deck line rise evenly towards both ends in a long sweep of equal unexaggerated proportions.

The hulls are also traditional. They have gently curved bilges and long, fine waterlines fore and aft. The boats are easily driven with a small low-powered engine. Many fishermen still use the traditional make-and-break gasoline engines, which have virtually disappeared elsewhere. They are fitted towards the aft end and are surrounded by the deckhouse for protection and easy access.

Newfoundland fishing boats are not powered by sails today, but it is not hard to imagine many with billowing canvases spread aloft. The hulls, with their flattering sheer, gently curved stem, and sloping transom and big outboard rudder have retained much of their sailing forebears' good looks. They are simple boats with no vices. They are truly versatile, adaptable to everything from squid-jigging (with automatic jiggers) to trap fishing, from lobstering to gillnetting.

Overleaf, left: Filled to the brim with capelin, this Cape Broyle, Nfld., boat is low in the water. The red-and-white boat in the background is Nova Scotian built, an increasingly common sight in Newfoundland.

Overleaf, right: Another decked-in boat at Bonavista. Interesting fittings are the car steering wheel on the front starboard corner of the deckhouse, and the capstan, which uses car tires to create a good grip.

The motionless waters of Brigus South, Nfld., cushion this small, tidy classic boat. It is partially decked over to store the catch, and is powered with an outboard motor, with oars for emergencies.

Facing page: Resting on the wharf at Comfort Cove, Nfld., is a similar but slightly larger boat. It has a small inboard engine.

Overleaf, left: A small white fleet of boats in New Bonaventure, Nfld., pay homage to the tradition of painting all the boats of one port the same colour—a tradition that seems to be dying out. Some of these boats have sculling oars protruding from the stern.

Overleaf, right: These clean boats in Cape Broyle, Nfld., speak of fishermen proud of their craft. The hole in the transom of the closest boat can take a sculling oar.

In these boats in Quidi Vidi, the slats beneath the thwarts prevent slippery fish from moving and affecting the boats' stability. The boats' stout construction can be seen in the large knees on the forward thwarts. Another example of individuality is the single thole pin; elsewhere in Atlantic Canada, boats are fitted with two thole pins.

Facing page: Alongside the Narrows of St. John's Harbour, opposite Signal Hill, boats lie under canvas and wait for better weather. Winter in Newfoundland, as elsewhere, means a reduction in fishing activity: boats are taken ashore, repaired, and repainted.

THE PRINCE EDWARD ISLAND SURFBOAT

Facing page: A quartet of surfboats in storage await summer. The sharp, raked stems and flat bottoms need only a touch of paint to make them ready for a season of protecting swimmers.

A lifeguard demonstrates how light a surfboat is as he prepares to take it out. The buoyancy compartments under the thwarts are permanent.

PRINCE EDWARD ISLAND surfboats are prevalent wherever shore conditions make it difficult to build safe harbours and there is a need to go to sea for supplies, for rescue services, or to fish. Sandy beaches, in particular, are not good for launching or retrieving boats because of breaking waves, so specialized vessels have been developed. These boats are located in diverse corners of the world, such as Australia, where east-coast lifeguards and their boats are well known; Pitcairn Island, where supplies and mail are still brought ashore by surfboats; Sable Island, where surfboats were in use until recently, when they were replaced by helicopters; Prince Edward Island; and on the beaches of the north shore of Nova Scotia, where they are as familiar as lifeguards.

Always white with bright-red trim, these boats are easily recognizable. Perhaps surprisingly, they are still made of wood. According to Parks Canada, the boats were built with cedar or redwood planking until 15 years ago. But the nine boats constructed during the winter of 1989, by Hutt Brothers of Alberton, P.E.I., were made of plywood planking. Somewhat similar in design to the New Jersey beach skiff, they are manufactured using wood on the Island and a special mold, to help preserve the skills that were once so much a part of Maritime coastal traditions.

The surfboat, like many other boat types, has been designed to fulfil a single purpose. About 4-1/2 feet by 14 feet, it has a flat bottom, which allows it to sit upright on the beach ready for instant use. The bottom is not too wide, so that the boat can be rowed easily and maintain good sea-keeping properties. Also, the curved sides allow the lifeguard to pull people over the sides safely and without tipping. The curved sides and the well-raked stem further assist the rower, by penetrating the shore waves.

The boat is strong but light, as it has to face onshore waves, which can be deceptively powerful over a gently sloping beach. This also makes it easy for a pair of lifeguards to carry the boat down the beach to the water's edge. The craft is built on steam-bent frames in clinker fashion; that is, the four side planks overlap. This type of construction was always used for wooden lifeboats, because the overlapping planks allow the boats to remain watertight, even though they spend most of their life out of the water. The clinker style also seems to make slightly steadier boats, as the edges of the planks act as tiny keels and help prevent rolling.

The interior of the surfboat is not unusual. There are three thwarts that have buoyant material beneath them, enhancing the safety of the boat. There are two pairs of oarlocks, which allow for a little more manoeuvrability for inexperienced rowers than traditional Maritime thole pins. The wide, flat transom can take an outboard motor, but no surfboats in the beach rescue service are powered.

It is hoped that surfboats will be in service for years to come as symbols of Prince Edward Island wooden-boat-building craftsmanship.

THE ROWING SHELL AND THE ST. JOHN'S ROYAL REGATTA

Facing page: **The carnival spirit invades St. John's, Nfld., every year at the annual regatta on Quidi Vidi Lake. The crowds are watching one of the boats speed by, or are the oarsmen watching the crowds speed by? It seems that the other boat is well ahead, or well behind, this six-man shell.**

THE ORGANIZERS OF THE St. John's Royal Regatta claim that it is the oldest annual sporting event in North America. Held on Quidi Vidi Lake, in St. John's, Nfld., it usually takes place on August 3, depending on the weather. The day of the regatta is a civic holiday, the only one whose date may be altered to suit the weather.

The first regatta took place in St. John's Harbour in 1818. Soon afterwards, its venue was moved to the calmer waters of Quidi Vidi. Today, men row up and down the 4,000-foot course, rounding a marker buoy—an unusual feature in rowing races—the women have to complete one direction. The hardy race crews of six men and a coxswain usually come from St. John's, but a few hail from outside communities. The female crews are not a recent phenomenon: records show that women were competing in this unique regatta as early as the 1880s.

The rowing shells themselves have fixed seats, not the more common sliding seat that has been used in competitive rowing for almost a century. There are nine rowing shells in the racing fleet: the five competitive shells, built by Simms Brothers in Toronto, Ont., date back to the early 1960s; the four practice boats, built in Kelowna, B.C., are even older.

The varnished wooden racing shells—or "sculls," as they are sometimes called—are 51 feet long. Somewhat wider than modern racing craft, they weigh 415 pounds. Newfoundland's H.H. Randell designed the first shells, based on English racing shells of the mid-1880s; the first craft were built in Newfoundland by Robert Sexton.

The rowers sit on the side opposite their oar, in a cockpit that is wider than the boat's hull. A deep keel acts as a strong backbone for the slender hull, and the rowers sit alternately on each side of it, on narrow thwarts with scraps of upholstery to cushion their ordeal. They brace their feet under a strap on a board fixed beneath the seat of the man behind them. The long oars, which have deeply dished blades, are pivoted through oarlocks on small, fixed metal outriggers. Because the rowers and oarlocks are on opposite sides of the wide cockpit, the outriggers are not so large as those of more modern sculls.

The shells are not so light as modern racing craft, but they are light when compared with other recreational boats. They have small frames and a strong cockpit with metal bracing at the stress areas. Every part of the structure performs its function while also adding strength to the vessel. For instance, the floor boards are longitudinal strength members, and so is the long cockpit side; the hull frames also frame the cockpit.

Because the boats have not changed radically over the years, rowing records have not been set that often. Times in all types of modern sporting events perhaps reflect the improvement in equipment more than the competitor's technique or ability. At the St. John's Royal Regatta, the record set by a crew in 1901 was not broken for 80 years. That crew was elected to the Canadian Sports Hall of Fame.

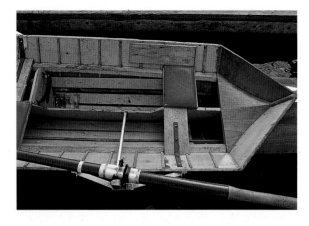

Looking into the forward end of the cockpit of a six-man boat, one can see the fixed seat, a unique feature of the Newfoundland rowing craft. The well-worn and patched appearance of the interior tells of a long, hard life. Because these craft are quite wide, the rowers sit on one side and pull their oar on the other.

Right: The boats may not be so slim as modern sliding-seat racing shells, but the slender lines of this boat can still be admired. It has been lowered into the water at a special slipway built for the St. John's Royal Regatta. The long oars lie at the ready.

Resting on the quiet waters of Quidi Vidi Harbour is an older type of competitive boat. This larger, heavier craft is sometimes used for practice. When the oarsmen transfer from this to the lighter shells, they find a remarkable change.

IMAGINATIVE BOATS

Facing page: The owner of this boat in North Rustico, P.E.I., is well prepared for heavy weather, but it would not be pleasant standing on the tiny foredeck pulling in an anchor while a force five blows! How many passengers will it sleep?

These little flat-bottomed boats in Buctouche, N.B., are identical and are used in a local regatta. The only way they can be distinguished is by their colour—and it pays to advertise.

THE URGE TO GO TO SEA seems to live in the heart of everyone close to the sound of a breaking wave. "Be it ever so humble, there's no boat like mine" could be the motto of these people. Their boats may not be to everyone's taste, but to their owners, they are the *Loveboat, Queen Mary, Santa Maria,* and *Britannia* rolled into one miniature dreamboat.

A boy's first watercraft may be as simple as a few boards or fishing boxes nailed together to form a crude raft. A single box for a tyke who should not be going to sea yet, as he is too small, and two or more for his older friend, who is bigger, more skilled, more daring, and more ambitious. From here, a boy can graduate to a "real" boat, which may be some derelict discarded in the corner of the harbour. It can be refurbished with a few nails, some bits of wood, and lots of hope.

Fishermen, on the other hand, do not usually indulge in flights of nautical whimsy. Theirs is a more serious quest, and nautical fancy usually stops at droll names. Many otherwise-purposeful boats sport appellations to show that the owner's humour transcends all the hard work and danger that usually accompanies him to the fishing grounds. Who can suppress a laugh at *Kostalot* or *Misinformed?* And the *Youno* is feeling *So-So* but *Might Go, Just 'n Time* for a *Little Dip! My Last One* is a *Mistake,* but *2 Late, Who Cares, You Go On!* All these are registered names. In the Canadian Register of Ships, Fishing Vessel Edition, Maritime vessels start with *A & K* and finish with *Zweelo.*

Then there is the other sailor, the one who ventures to sea only when it is calm, sunny, and safe—the pleasure boatman who cannot afford the fibreglass or aluminum craft of the nautical designers who create floating visions. What does he take to sea?

His boat is usually small, ill proportioned, and lacking in aesthetic balance, but it is often well cared for, spotless, and painted in cheery, carefree colours and styles. It may be used occasionally for a little sport fishing or to go from Point A to Point B. This boat seems to have no purpose but to please its owner. In this, it surely succeeds.

Facing page: This dory in Dark Harbour, Grand Manan Island, N.B., is going to scare the fish. Perhaps the owner was a sailor on sub-chasers in the Second World War. Let's hope that he does not meet an amorous (or angry) great white shark.

What a simple, practical way to get a small pram to the water. The hydrodynamics will be affected somewhat, but this is not a boat that moves fast, anyway. Other uses for this craft: a trailer or wheel-barrow.

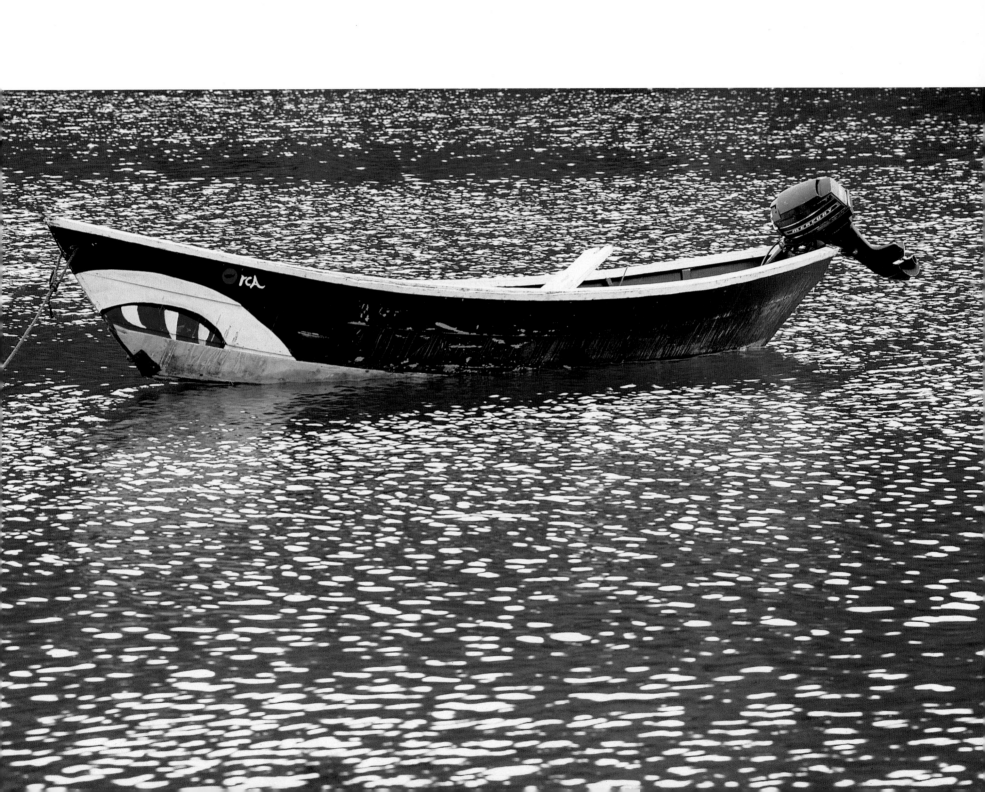

Take two fish boxes, nail them together end to end, arrange two planks in V-formation at one end, nail on a seat, and presto, Stage 2 in marine transport. There seems to be a production line in Sambro, N.S.

Facing page: This Tidnish boat has no frills. It looks as if a twist has crept into the structure somewhere. Back to the drawing board.

This tiny, forlorn flat-bottomed boat placidly waits for her owner to bail her out, fix the leak, and repaint her the bright blue she once was.

Glossary

Aft Towards the *stern*, or back, of a boat.

Beam The breadth of a boat at the widest point.

Bilge The lowest part of the inside of a boat.

Bow The forward part of a boat.

Brail To empty a seine net by tightening the line at the bottom and "pursing" the circular net, trapping the fish.

Capstan A marine type of vertical drum winch for hauling anchors, nets, cargo, etc.

Carvel built The outer-planking method used when the planks are laid edge to edge, producing a smooth surface (see *clinker built*).

Chine The angle or line where the sides and bottom of a V- or flat-bottomed boat meet.

Clinker built The outer-planking method where the lower edge of each plank overlaps the upper edge of the plank below it. Sometimes known as clench or lapstrake planking.

Coaming The raised wooden piece around the edge of the deck of a boat.

Cuddy A small cabin or cookhouse in the forward part of a boat, below decks.

Davit A small crane or derrick used to lift light weights aboard a boat.

Deckhouse A small cabin erected on a deck of a boat. Does not extend the full breadth of the vessel.

Dope A type of paint used to waterproof canvas of a light boat or canoe.

Fore Towards the *bow*, or front, of a boat.

Forecastle The space beneath the forward deck of a boat.

Forefoot The intersection between the *keel* and the curved section of a boat. A cutaway *forefoot* has the angle of the *keel* increased towards the *stem* to make the boat easier to turn and to haul out of the water.

Freeboard The vertical distance from the waterline to the upper edge of the *gunwale* usually measured at midships.

Gantry A type of derrick or lifting frame to support various types of fishing gear.

Gunwale The upper edge of the side of a boat.

Hull The body of a boat, exclusive of masts, engines, equipment, rigging, etc.

Keel The lowest structural member of a boat, the backbone, running *fore* and *aft* on the centreline.

Oarlock A swivelling crutch on the side of a boat to support an oar for rowing.

Outrigger An extension frame out from the side of a boat to support oars, rigging, or a small auxiliary hull.

Port The left side of a boat when facing forward.

Rib The frame of a boat running from the *keel* to the *gunwale*.

Rudder A wide piece of metal or wood, hinged at the *stern* of a boat. Used to turn or change the boat's direction.

Sculling Originally, to propel a boat by working a single oar through a hole or notch in the *transom*. Recently, also refers to working a pair of oars in a light craft.

Sheer The upward curve of the line of a boat's *gunwale* towards the *bow* and the *stern*.

Skeg An extension of the after end of the *keel*, to hold and protect the lower end of the *rudder*.

Skiff A small boat, usually *clinker built* and flat bottomed for propulsion by oars.

Snatch block A block with a single sheave and a hinged opening above the sheave to take the rope. This eliminates the need to thread the whole length of rope through the block.

Starboard The right side of a boat when facing forward.

Stem The foremost timber of a boat where the two sides meet.

Stern The after part of a boat.

Stringer A *fore* and *aft* strength timber in a boat, a type of girder.

Thole Pin A wooden pin fitted vertically in a hole in the *gunwale* to keep the oar in place when rowing. Usually used in pairs with the oar placed between them.

Thwart The transverse wooden bench or seat in a boat.

Tombstone The name used for the *transom* in a dory, because of its similarity in shape.

Transom The transverse planking that forms the after end of a square-sterned boat.

Wheelhouse The deckhouse on a larger boat from which it is steered and navigated.

Yaw To go from side to side, off course.

Yawl A sailing rig with two masts where the after or mizzen mast is smallest and stepped *aft* of the *rudder* post.